Menta... Issues in Schools

A Guide for Teachers, School Administrators, and Parents

By Meg Muckenhoupt, Sc.M.

**Health and Human Development Programs
Education Development Center, Inc.**

Table of Contents

The Extent of the Problem

Between six and nine million children and adolescents in the United States have serious emotional disorders that substantially limit their ability to function in their families, schools, and communities.[1,2,3] As many as 8 percent of adolescents are clinically depressed; up to 2 percent of adolescents have obsessive-compulsive disorder, and 3 percent have an eating disorder.[2]

Adolescent mental illness can be deadly. Suicide is the third-leading cause of death for teenagers, after accidents and homicide, and more than 90 percent of adolescents who commit suicide have a mental disorder.*[2,73] Teenagers with major depression are 12 times more likely to die by suicide than their peers. The rate of death for teens with anorexia nervosa from suicide, starvation, or electrolyte imbalance is 12 times that of normal peers.[2]

Apart from emotional pain, mental illness has a devastating effect on teenagers' schoolwork, their health, and their future. Fourteen percent of high school dropouts have a mental illness.[1]

---

*Published data on adolescent rates of death from suicide and homicide vary with the age range considered. The statistics in this monograph reflect the data available from the National Center for Injury Prevention and Control (NCIPC) Web site[73], which lists the top three causes of death for adolescents ages 13–19 in 1998 (the most recent year available) as:

1 Unintentional Injury	7,436
2 Homicide and Legal Intervention	2,486
3 Suicide	1,984

Many reports on youth death rates focus on broader age ranges. The NCIPC's book on youth violence prevention states that in 1997, 3,700 Americans under the age of 19 were murdered,[25] while the American Association for Suicidology reported that over 4,000 Americans ages 15–24 completed suicide in 1998.[21]

All sources agree that homicide and suicide are the second- and third-leading causes of death among American teenagers. The prevalence of violent death among youth is tragic, and directly linked to mental illness. Many types of dating and domestic abuse are highly correlated with mental illness. For example, a recent study by the researchers at the Harvard School of Public Health showed that one in five female high school students in Massachusetts reported being physically or sexually abused by a dating partner. These girls were three times more likely than their peers to show signs of eating disorders, and eight times more likely to attempt suicide in a given year.[74]

Domestic violence, child neglect, and verbal abuse are all violent stressors in many teenagers' lives. However, interventions to reduce these types of violence are far beyond most schools' abilities and mission, and beyond the scope of this monograph.

Adolescents with untreated emotional disorders are at a heightened risk for contracting HIV through unprotected sex.[3] Mental illness also plays a role in teen drug and alcohol abuse: About half the people ages 15–24 who have mental illnesses abuse drugs or alcohol, and drug and alcohol use has been linked to anxiety disorders, depression, and suicide.[2,4,5] Having an anxiety disorder or depression doubles one's risk of becoming dependent on drugs or alcohol.[6]

The good news is that most mental illnesses—including depression, bipolar disorder, anxiety disorders, and schizophrenia—are treatable, with high rates of recovery. Unfortunately, most victims do not get the help they need, commonly because they fear that others will discover their problems, or they believe that "nothing will help" (see "Denial," pg. 4).[7]

Although most high schools do provide individual counseling, they do not necessarily have the staff to identify all students with psychiatric illnesses, much less counsel them. Nationwide, there is one school psychologist for every 1,930 students, and just one school counselor for every 560 students—more than twice what the American Counseling Association recommends.[8,9,10] In some areas of the country, the ratio of students to school psychologists rises to more than 7,000 to 1.[9]

Students with mental illness can survive and succeed in school, but they are more likely to do so when staff can detect these students' symptoms, refer students to treatment, and accommodate their disabilities in the classroom.

What Is Mental Illness?

According to the National Alliance for the Mentally Ill, "Mental illnesses are physical brain disorders that profoundly disrupt a person's ability to think, feel, and relate to others and their environment."[11] Common disorders include the following:[2,12]

♦ **Depression:** Overwhelming unhappiness, hopelessness, and a lack of interest in life

♦ **Bipolar disorder:** Depression alternating with mania, an intensely energetic or irritable mood, with poor judgment and self-control

♦ **Schizophrenia:** A "split" from reality, often involving distorted or "flattened" emotions, paranoia, hallucinations, and poor attention

♦ **Obsessive-compulsive disorder:** Engaging in rituals, such as hand-washing or counting to high numbers, to dispel paralyzing anxieties

♦ **Anxiety disorders:** Fears of common situations (such as crowds), which are so powerful that they grossly limit victims' lives; "panic attacks" are a common anxiety disorder

♦ **Eating Disorders:** An obsession with eating, weight, or dieting that results in dangerous activities like self-starvation, binge-eating, or vomiting

Warning Signs

Most students will never become mentally ill. However, many students will experience profound disruptions in their lives, whether due to mental illness; academic difficulties; personal or family troubles; personal crises like sexual assault, a death in the family, or a dramatic change in one's financial situation; or a global crisis like an act of terrorism. Their behavior and academic work can abruptly deteriorate. These students often approach teachers

and staff for help; you may also decide to intervene before a
student admits to having problems.

Although teachers and staff can suggest strategies for improving
academic performance, some students need professional counseling. It is important to **recognize** the signs that a student is overwhelmed, **know** what services are available, and **refer** students to
counseling or urgent care when needed.

Denial

It can be difficult and painful for people who are close to a
teenager to recognize the onset of mental illness. Families and
friends often deny teenagers' mental illnesses, claiming that symptoms are just a "phase." Parents may not want their child labeled
"mentally ill."[3] They may also feel too overwhelmed by the problem to cope with it at all.

Students also have strong motivation to deny their illnesses. The
stigma attached to psychiatric disorders is immense; it is a terrible
burden for students who are trying to begin their adult lives.[13] In
order to conceal their problems from future employers and college
admissions committees, some students will avoid contact with
mental health services until their symptoms are severe. They may
try to mute or hide their symptoms through "self-medication"—
usually with alcohol or street drugs, which carry the risk of
addiction.

Mixed Signals

There are few pure cases of mental illness in adolescents.
Depressed and bipolar teens may also show signs of attention
deficit/hyperactivity disorder, substance abuse, anxiety disorders,
or aggressive "externalizing" behaviors.[14,15] Up to 50 percent of
adolescents who have any one psychiatric diagnosis have at least
two or more disorders.[16]

Symptoms of adolescent mental illness may also be different from
those of adults. Adolescents with depression show many more
symptoms of anxiety, such as fear of separation from their families,
and bodily symptoms, such as stomachaches and headaches, than

do depressed adults.[2] Adolescents seem irritable, rather than sad and melancholic.[14]

No single symptom distinguishes students who are in crisis from their peers. Rather, it is patterns of sudden, marked changes in the student's mood or behavior that can indicate that a student is suffering from mental illness. The following symptoms, in particular, should be cause for concern:[2,17,18,19]

♦ **References to suicide or homicide: All** suicide threats are serious. No matter what the context, a student who talks about committing suicide is at risk and needs to be evaluated by a mental health professional as soon as possible. Most people planning to commit suicide talk about it first (for more information, see "Suicide," pg. 6.) Threats against others also demand immediate response (see "Violence," pg. 10).

♦ **Problems with academic work:** Absenteeism or decreased quality of work and withdrawal from class participation and discussions can be signs of distress. Problems can manifest themselves in many ways. Students may show an inability to concentrate, seem preoccupied, or have memory lapses. They may become restless, fall asleep during lectures, or behave inappropriately and disrupt class. Students going through a manic episode may finish their schoolwork quickly and creatively but in a very disorganized way.

♦ **Changes in mood:** Crying spells, angry outbursts, hypersensitivity, irritability, and carelessness—such as impulsiveness or excessive risk-taking—are all danger signs. Some students become paralyzed by anxiety before tests and experience a racing pulse, shortness of breath, and a sense of impending doom.

♦ **Physical changes:** Sudden changes in a student's sleep patterns, weight, appetite, or energy level (being constantly tired, or the converse—acting wired) can all indicate distress, as can certain physical complaints, such as frequent headaches, gastrointestinal troubles, or dizziness. Signs of eating disorders—e.g., vomiting after meals, uncontrollable dieting or bingeing—may indicate a serious, complicated condition that should be treated as quickly as possible.

- ◆ **Changes in behavior:** Suicide threats are not the only sign of distress. Impaired communication—e.g., garbled speech, or disjointed, irrational conversations—can indicate that help is needed. Withdrawal from social interactions, excessive worrying, and general disorientation all point to psychological distress.

- ◆ **Losing contact with reality:** Some students have auditory or visual hallucinations, or become unable to tell fantasy from reality. They may begin acting strangely based on their delusions, or simply perform acts that are inappropriate to the social setting.

- ◆ **Substance abuse:** Although drug and alcohol abuse in and of itself is a major problem confronting students, it can also mask psychological distress.

- ◆ **Isolation:** Students may stop seeing long-time friends, or spend large amounts of time alone.

- ◆ **Lack of interest** in hobbies or social activities.

Suicide

uicide is the third-leading cause of death for teenagers, after accidents and homicide, and the rate of suicide attempts increases throughout the teen years.[2] Nearly 2,000 Americans ages 13–19 completed suicide in 1998; the majority of these young adults died via gunshot wounds.[21,73] Completed suicides are relatively rare, but suicide attempts are not; studies indicate that anywhere from 3 to 9 percent of high school students have attempted suicide.[22] Unfortunately, nearly 50 percent of adolescents do not recognize common signs of a peers' intention to commit suicide.[20]

The fact that suicide attempts are so common is a very, very good reason why **all** members of a school community, including students, should be trained to recognize and respond to suicidal students.[23] Distressed students who recognize the signs of suicidal intention in themselves or a friend may confide in many people other than the school psychologist, such as their parents, their friends, or a friendly cafeteria worker, bus driver, or school secretary. Unfortunately, many adults are not comfortable discussing suicide. Their awkward responses can be interpreted as rejection or disapproval by depressed suicidal teens, who may see this as one more piece of evidence that the world is against them and then finalize their suicide plans.[23] Same-age friends are often confused and disturbed by a suicide plan; they may not know where to get help for a suicidal friend, or they may agree to keep a secret, without comprehending that suicidal teens often die or severely injure themselves.

Once a suicidal student has been identified, that student must be referred to professional counseling immediately, before a suicide attempt takes place, and the student's parents should be contacted. If a school discovers that a student is suicidal and does not take action to prevent the suicide, that school may be sued by the student's family.[23] Running **any** sort of suicide prevention program without ensuring students' access to counseling services, creating a crisis management plan, and planning post-intervention procedures is highly irresponsible and can lead to lawsuits.[23]

Suicide Myths [23,24]

Myth: You can't stop someone from committing suicide if he or she really wants to do it. Most people who are considering suicide do not want to die; they just want the pain to stop. The impulse to kill themselves does **not** last forever.

Myth: You should never use the word "suicide" when talking with teens, because it will put the idea in their heads. Today's adolescents have many, many opportunities to learn about suicide outside the classroom—from family members or friends who have attempted suicide, or from books, movies, television, and music. Being honest with teenagers and saying the word can help them verbalize their feelings and talk about their despair.

Myth: Teenagers who talk about suicide never attempt suicide. On the contrary, more than 90 percent of suicidal adolescents give cues, or tell at least one other person about their intentions.

Warning Signs of Suicidal Thinking [7,18,19,23,24]

Below is a brief list of cues that a teenager may be considering suicide. Though each is a cause for some concern, no one symptom necessarily indicates suicidal intention. However, a pattern of several changes is an indication that a teenager is in trouble (for a more complete list of warning signs, see "Resources," pg. 31).

♦ Sudden changes in social patterns: Withdrawal from friends; starting to break rules or argue with adults.

♦ Attempts to put personal affairs in order, make amends for bad deeds, and give away prized possessions.

♦ Expressing a wish to die.

♦ Sudden improvement after a span of depression, often overnight: Many suicidal teenagers suddenly become cheerful once they have made a concrete plan to commit suicide in the immediate future.[23]

Talking to a Suicidal Teenager [23]

If you discover that a teenager is considering suicide, you are facing a crisis.[23] You need to make rapid decisions about how to get help for that student. Whenever possible, get a professional trained in crisis management, such as a mental health clinician, to work with you to figure out what to do to keep the student from killing him- or herself.[23]

Rather than direct statements like "I am thinking of taking my life," many suicidal teens make indirect comments like "Soon I'll be going home," "I'm tired of feeling this way," or "I'll show everyone how serious I am." **Always** ask teens to clarify what they mean by this kind of statement. Do not assume you know what he or she means. Suicidal teenagers often have problems talking about their feelings and asking for support. Do not minimize the importance of the teen's message; if a teenager is in pain and considering suicide, his or her feelings are **very** important.[23]

Also, don't underestimate the importance of being a good listener. Sometimes, simply talking about the problem will help students see that there are alternatives to their self-destructive actions.

When you are talking to a suicidal teenager, be nonjudgmental. Statements like "Suicide is wrong" or "I felt that way, and I didn't commit suicide" are belittling, as these students often feel like they have no other choice.[23] Ask questions to assess how much danger the student is in, such as the following:

♦ "What has made life so difficult?" The more problems the student names, the greater the risk.

♦ "How long have you been thinking about suicide? How often do you think about it?" The longer the time named, the greater the risk. Remember the acronym FID (**F**requency, **I**ntensity, and **D**uration) and ask questions accordingly.

♦ "Do you have a suicide plan?" The more detailed the plan, the greater the risk. If the student names a gun or knife, ask if the student has the weapon right then; if so, see if the student will leave it with you. **Never** try to disarm a teenager yourself. Instead, call the police or a crisis center.

♦ "Do you have any friends or family members that you regret hurting or leaving behind?" If the student has problems naming a friend or family member who is worth living for, the risk is great. If the student does name someone, get the name, address, and phone number of this person (or persons) and enlist their help.[23]

Dealing with a Suicide Crisis

A suicidal teen may need to make an emergency visit to a counselor, be hospitalized, or have a "suicide watch" organized by friends and family, depending on the degree of risk involved. **Always** consult a professional mental health worker before deciding on a course of action, if at all possible (see "Crisis Management," pg. 11).

Parents need to be notified immediately if their child is at risk for suicide. In some cases, parents will refuse to come and meet their child, and demand that school staff leave their child alone and stop trying to help. These parents may be denying that their child has a problem, or are apprehensive about the situation. Even if parents are uncooperative, school personnel's responsibility is clear: **Never** let an adolescent at risk for suicide leave school alone.[23]

Violence

In 1998, nearly 2,500 Americans ages 13–19 were murdered.[73] Ten percent of all public schools reported at least one serious violent crime to police or law enforcement in 1999, and nearly a million U.S. students took guns to school in 1998.[26] In 1994, the rate of violent victimization of juveniles ages 12–17 was nearly three times the adult rate, and almost one-third of those incidents were committed by schoolmates.[27]

More than 75 percent of secondary school students have either been victims of violence or witnessed acts of violence at home or at school.[28] Exposure to violence can increase the rate of many mental illnesses, including post-traumatic stress disorder, depression, and anxiety disorders.[28]

Warning Signs of Violence and "Profiling"

Wearing a trenchcoat or black clothing, listening to certain music, or reading certain books do **not** make a high school student a candidate for committing school violence, any more than having dark skin or a foreign accent makes a person a murderer.[27] Early warning signs are just that—signs that a student needs help, **not** a guarantee that a student will commit violence.[29]

Below are a few principles to keep in mind when dealing with students who may commit violence:[29]

♦ Do no harm. You should be identifying teens at risk of violence in order to help them, not to exclude, punish, or isolate them. Suspending a student who already feels alienated from school may just make things worse.

♦ Do not overreact to single words or incidents. Most students at risk for committing violence show multiple warning signs, over and over again, with increasing intensity.

♦ Avoid stereotypes about students' socioeconomic status, academic ability, or physical appearance.

♦ Understand the student's social context. Some acts are a result of factors in a student's home, school, or community environment.

Warning Signs of Violence [29,71]

Below is an **incomplete** list of signs warning that a student may commit violence at school (for a more complete listing, see "Resources," pg. 31):

♦ Social withdrawal, often from feelings of depression, rejection, persecution, or unworthiness

♦ Excessive feelings of rejection, isolation, or persecution

♦ Being a victim of violence or sexual abuse

♦ Expression of violence in writings and drawings

♦ Uncontrolled anger, frequently expressed in response to minor incidents

♦ Serious threats of violence, in particular, detailed and specific threats

Having a strong communication network will keep students from "falling through the cracks." The various groups can compare observations, determine whether a behavior has been recurring, and discuss how the campus community has dealt with the behavior in the past.[7] For example, a student who cuts herself might be seen by the police, the medical unit, and a school counselor, or she may be simply observed by a teacher, depending on the severity of her wounds. If a student has a detailed plan to hurt others, or is carrying a weapon and threatening to use it, both the student's parents and law enforcement need to be alerted **immediately.**

Crisis Management

Most schools have plans for dealing with fires, natural disasters, and student violence. A student's completed suicide, suicide attempt, or psychiatric hospitalization can have just as devastating an effect on the school community. Institutions need to develop plans to get police and paramedics to the scene of a crisis quickly and to get the student psychologically evaluated as soon as possible.[7]

Within a few hours of a suicide attempt at school, half the student body will know about it. School staff need to have a procedure in place to make sure that all faculty and staff have access to the same information about the event and can direct students, parents, and staff to counseling, as well as to people who can talk about the student, the student's suicide attempt, and the school's safety procedures. Having a single individual to answer questions and address the media will help keep rumors in check (for more information about creating a crisis plan or dealing with the media in the wake of a suicide, see "Resources," pg. 31).

In any psychological emergency, a student's friends and classmates will wonder, "What could I have done to prevent this?" It is important to give members of the campus community a chance to talk about what happened with counseling staff as soon as possible after a crisis, especially a completed suicide. The effects of a crisis "ripple" out to the campus community, affecting student groups or sports teams the student may have been involved in, faculty and staff who had contact with the student or witnessed the crisis, etc.[7,29]

After a crisis, teenagers are likely to express their grief, fear, and guilt by reporting vague physical symptoms, such as stomachaches, and may stop doing chores or schoolwork. They may withdraw from social contact, start disrupting their classes, or begin to experiment with drugs and alcohol. Older teenagers may feel unable to handle their adult responsibilities, and start to feel guilty and helpless.[30] It is important to help parents, teachers, and staff understand students' reactions to the crisis and get grief counseling for themselves as well.[29]

Administrators need to make sure that **all** staff at the school who deal with crises understand what has happened and what is being done to keep future crises from occurring.

Referring Students to Counseling

Most students who show signs of mental illness will not experience a mental health crisis at school. Nevertheless, there are several situations in which you should refer students to a mental health professional:[31,32,33,34,35,36,37]

♦ The student needs more help than you can give: Threats of suicide or violence against others, eating disorders, and severe psychological distress require professional treatment. Staff members who overextend themselves by offering "therapy on the fly" to severely disturbed students help no one. You may wish to ask the student's permission before calling and then schedule the appointment while the student is with you (see "Confidentiality and Consent," pg. 16).

♦ You feel overwhelmed, stressed, or uncomfortable dealing with the situation yourself: Even in less dire circumstances, staff may not feel comfortable trying to help a student whose mother has recently died, or whose panic attacks keep the student from attending class.

♦ The student seems highly agitated or enraged: Students who are overwhelmed by their emotions will need time to "vent" before they can calm down and regain control. These students need to see a mental health clinician immediately. If you feel comfortable, give the student time to "vent" his or her feelings. Do not try to argue with the student's conclusions or ask too many questions; the idea is to support the student and give him or her time to calm down before help arrives, or as you walk to the counseling center together. However, to ensure your own safety, as well as the student's well-being, leave the room if there is **any** indication of danger, and then contact the student's parents and the designated member of the school's crisis management team (or, if your school has not designated such a person, contact the principal).[33]

♦ The student seems suicidal: These students should also see a mental health professional immediately. Ask questions to assess the student's level of risk. If possible, accompany the student to the counseling center; you should never leave an adolescent at risk for suicide alone.[23] Finally, notify the student's parents, as well as the school's crisis management team.

Before you make a referral, learn what resources your school and community have to offer. Your school may not offer any counseling services for seriously disturbed students and may instead rely on community hospitals or social service agencies for student mental health care. Find out the answers to the following questions:

♦ Does the school offer counseling, or do students need to go to a community counseling center for help? If the latter, where is the nearest center?

♦ What are its hours?

♦ What services does the center offer?

♦ How long is the waiting list? Will the student have to wait weeks for treatment?

♦ Does the center offer urgent care appointments every day? If not, where should students go in emergencies? Who can escort students at risk of harming themselves or others to a hospital?

Ideally, schools should assemble a list of resources offered by the school and the community. If the school refers students to a local counseling center, the center should provide a short guide with information on its services, phone numbers, and its policy on urgent and after-hours care.

Tips on Making a Referral [23,33,34,35,36,37]

Students may have a variety of reasons for not wanting to see a counselor. Approaching these students calmly, with compassion, can help them get the treatment they need. Here are some suggestions:

♦ Express your concern for the student's welfare and your desire to help the student solve his or her problems.

♦ Be specific about what **behaviors** concern you, for example, missed classes, poor work, or crying in class. Do not make generalizations about the student's personality, like "You've been getting lazy." Keep good records of the student's behavior and of your interactions with that student.

♦ Be clear and direct. Instead of saying, "I think you could use some help," say, "It sounds like you're going through a very difficult time, and it's affecting your work. I think a counselor could help you."

♦ Tell the student that it is not a sign of weakness to see a counselor. Let the student know that it takes strength and courage for people to get the help they need, and that things can improve.

♦ Emphasize that counseling is confidential (if that is the case—see "Confidentiality and Consent," pg. 16). However, do say that you will not tell anyone else about the student's problem. Although many teenagers are eager to extract these promises, it is against the law—and morally wrong—to withhold information if students are in danger of hurting themselves or others (see "Confidentiality and Consent," pg. 16).

♦ If applicable, explain that there are many types of help available at the counseling center, such as support groups, "how to study" groups, or treatment for eating disorders.

♦ Unless the student clearly needs emergency treatment, leave the option open for the student to refuse counseling now and reconsider it later.

Follow-Up

It is a good idea to follow up on a student's referral with the student's parents, both to show your support and interest and to make sure that the student actually followed through with the referral.[37] However, as therapists are not allowed to divulge information about a student's treatment (see "Consent," pg. 17), you will need to ask the student directly, or the student's parents, if he or she has started therapy. Student may not follow up on a referral for a variety of reasons, for example, the student may not be ready to get help, or the local counseling center may not offer treatment the students wants or expects. If you discover that a student has not followed up on your referral, you have several options if you wish to continue to help the student seek treatment:[23]

♦ If the student is not ready to get help, you should accept that, but encourage the student to consider other options. Emphasize that you can only give limited assistance. Continue to check in with the student until the student is ready to see a counselor.

♦ If the counseling center is not accessible to the student due to scheduling conflicts, help the student find another counselor or center.

♦ If the counselor did not understand the student's needs, ask the student's parents for permission to talk to the counselor directly, to give the counselor more information.

♦ If the student did not "click" with the counselor because of a personality or culture clash, encourage the student to see another counselor or go to another counseling service.

Confidentiality and Consent

Confidentiality

Sooner or later, most teachers will encounter a student who says, "My parents would kill me if they found out how I'm feeling. Promise me you won't tell anyone!" Teenagers are **very** concerned about confidentiality, with good reason. Nobody wants their peers, future employers, military recruiters, or college admissions officers talking about their treatment. Concerns about confidentiality are one of the major barriers to adolescents seeking mental health services.[38,39]

Unfortunately, certain situations demand that teachers tell students' secrets. All 50 states require teachers, counselors, and mental health professionals to report suspected cases of child abuse and neglect if they are reasonably certain that neglect has taken place.[40] If the student who says "My parents would kill me" is in physical danger, you do not have a choice. According to mandatory reporting laws, you **must** report the danger to the appropriate school administrator, Child Protective Services office, or state authority.[40] These same laws also apply to teenage parents who abuse their own children.

Similarly, if a teenager threatens to hurt him- or herself or someone else, therapists are required to take action to prevent the threat from being carried out. Teachers should notify the student's parents or school counseling staff. In Virginia, for example, anyone "licensed as administrative or instructional personnel by the board of education" who believes a student is at risk for suicide **must** contact the student's parents to ask if they are aware of the student's mental state and if they wish to get counseling for the student.[41]

These are the only two exceptions; in all other circumstances you should respect a student's confidentiality. Do not discuss a student's personal problems with colleagues, or refer to the student's problems in public places (such as the cafeteria or the school parking lot). Remember that although the student's difficulties are obvious to you, other members of the community may not know anything about them—and probably do not need to know about them. If a student has trusted you with confidential, personal information, respect that trust by keeping the information to yourself.

These confidentiality guidelines do not apply to students' disruptive or destructive behaviors. In cases where there may be a need for disciplinary action, talk with administrators and mental health staff who may be confronting similar behavior by the student in different situations.

Consent

Successful therapy for minors usually involves collaboration between school systems, mental health processionals, and parents.[42,43] Most parents are essential contributors to their children's recovery.[44] School districts that do not clearly ask for parental consent before providing health services or therapy to the student have been attacked by furious parents—and rightly so.[40,45] To help students get the treatment they need—and to avoid lawsuits— teachers and staff **must** talk to parents and obtain their consent. Here are four likely scenarios:

♦ In some states, minors can themselves consent to mental health care, at least for the first few sessions, but this varies according to local statutes.[46] However, most adolescents are below the age where they can legally seek therapy without consulting a parent or guardian. This age generally varies from 16 to 18, depending on the state and the type of counseling the adolescent is seeking; standards vary enormously from state to state.[42,47] In most cases, a counselor **must** gain consent from a parent before beginning therapy with a minor.

♦ Some adolescents are considered "emancipated" or "mature" minors, because of a judicial decree, marriage, or military service, and may consent to treatment by themselves. If you suspect that a distressed student is an emancipated minor, it is best to discuss the student's status and your reporting obligations with a school counselor or psychologist.

♦ In the case of children whose parents are divorced, usually only the custodial parent can give or withhold consent to treatment.[42]

♦ Students in crisis may receive emergency treatment without parental consent, just as in a physical emergency.

Therapists and counselors generally may not release any information about a minor's treatment unless the parent or guardian has given them specific written permission to do so—and even then, the therapist may be reluctant to compromise the student's privacy. If you wish to know if a student has started therapy, ask the student or the student's parents.

Prevention

Schools are in the business of education, not treating mental illness. However, illnesses like depression, bipolar disorder, and schizophrenia can make it impossible for students to attend to the business of learning. The symptoms of these disorders, such as fatigue and exhaustion, inability to concentrate, nausea, and hallucinations, can make it all but impossible for students to pay attention in class, finish their homework, and work cooperatively with their peers. Given the enormous number of teenagers who are impaired by mental illness, schools must add some form of prevention to their tasks in order to help students learn.[47]

There are vast quantities of research on preventing adolescent suicide and mental illness and on averting school violence.[44,48,49,50,51] From this body of knowledge, two conclusions are certain. First, the entire school community needs to be able to recognize warning signs that a youth is in trouble.[29] Second, designing a brief, one-shot program to combat one specific disorder is ineffective; multi-year programs have a better chance of changing the lives of at-risk teens.[51]

In general, short-term programs produce short-term benefits. Ongoing programs to help at-risk students with several different types of life skills in different contexts are far more effective.[29]

Programs that treat only the child are bound to fail. Any plan for prevention needs to include input from parents and other family members, students, and the community; as students who are having problems at school are probably also having trouble dealing with their family and their community as well.[29] For example, there may be particular environments or conditions that "set off" the symptoms and harmful behavior.[29]

Effective prevention programs can teach students self-management, conflict-resolution, and social problem-solving skills, as well as how to seek social support. Parents can master new skills in parenting and communication, teachers can acquire more cooperative-learning techniques, and school staff can learn how to build their school's capacity for change.

Types of Prevention

For most schools, there are three main levels of intervention:

♦ Universal prevention, which involves a whole population (the entire school)

♦ Selective intervention, which targets individuals or groups that are at an increased risk of developing disorders (e.g., children from poor families or whose parents have a mental illness)

♦ Indicated interventions, which are carried out with people who have some signs of mental illness but have not yet developed a full-blown syndrome[51,52]

Each of these approaches has its advantages and its drawbacks. Universal programs keep participants from being labeled as "crazy" or "weak" by their peers and school staff. However, most of the participants in universal programs are healthy students who will not go on to develop mental illnesses in any case. The universal interventions themselves are usually not intensive, and may not significantly alter the participants' lives.[51] On the other hand, the price of lost education, lost productivity, and emotional toll on families from undiagnosed mental illness is so great that even mild interventions may be worthwhile. Selective and indicated interventions are more expensive and intensive, but can have longer-lasting effects.

Prevention and Public Space

Changes in a school's social structure and physical appearance can help students feel safe and can prevent violence. These are a few ways to make a school safer:[29]

♦ Make the amount of time students spend in crowded hallways as short as possible, for example, by staggering lunch and dismissal times.

♦ Have adults visible throughout the building, for example, by encouraging parents to visit the school.

♦ Prohibit students from gathering in hard-to-supervise areas of the school, like back stairways.

♦ Designate a specific area within the grounds or buildings where students can sit quietly.[53]

A school's physical environment can also affect whether students are willing to go to a counselor or psychologist. It is important to have a quiet place where students can talk privately, without interruptions or distractions.

Prevention and School-Based Clinics: Access to Care

Any population of teenage students will include people who are experiencing psychological distress. To help students keep their symptoms under control and their studies on-track, students need to be able to get care when they need it. One solution is to have mental health services located at or near a school, in either an on-campus clinic or at a nearby health center "owned" by the school administration.

There are more than 1,300 school-based or school-linked clinics in the United States, which have become the "de facto" mental health system for adolescents.[45,54] More than 11 million children and adolescents in the United States have no health insurance and little access to health care outside their schools.[45] Seventy percent of teens who become mentally ill do not get any formal treatment outside of school.[2,54] Providing services in schools increases students' access to treatment. Some studies show that students who report mental health symptoms at school-based or -linked clinics were more likely to receive treatment than if they went to other providers.[2,39]

Close to half the students who come to school-based clinics are seeking help with social or psychological concerns, such as problems with their families or peers, drug or alcohol use, emotional distress, or physical or sexual abuse.[8,47] Having the center at school cuts travel time, a major obstacle to teens and their families using services, and provides counseling staff with an opportunity to observe students' behavior in class and with their peers—giving them a much broader and more accurate view of the students' abilities and impairments than they would get from a traditional office visit.[39]

Several federal agencies, including the Centers for Disease Control and Prevention (through its Adolescent School Health Project), have supported preventive programming and integrating mental health services into secondary schools.[61] (For more information about school health services, see "Resources," pg. 31.)

Prevention and Stress

Stress is "any situation that evokes negative thoughts and feelings in a person."[32] Reducing chronic stress ameliorates symptoms for people with mental illness, and helps all students concentrate and work to the best of their ability.

Either too much **or** too little stress will keep a student from learning: Too little stress is boring, too much stress is overwhelming.[33] At most schools, though, the problem for students is how to reduce stress.

Studies show that stress increases when people feel like they do not have control over their lives.[2] Giving students a sense of control over their academic lives can dramatically reduce their stress levels.[32,35] Here are some suggestions:

♦ Test students regularly, instead of having a single big exam at the end of the course.

♦ Give students individual feedback about their work and what they can do to improve it.

♦ Make your expectations clear.

♦ Give students some choices as to what courses to take.

♦ Tell students the purpose of their assignments.

♦ Ask for their feedback on courses.

♦ Provide a clear reward system for excellent performance.

Accommodating Students with Psychiatric Disabilities

Students with psychiatric disabilities are not intellectually disabled; instead, their cognitive processes, like short-term memory and the ability to concentrate, may be affected. They can suffer from a variety of symptoms that affect their schoolwork, some of which are caused by the illness, and some of which are side-effects of psychiatric medication. Common problems include the following:[56]

♦ **Inability to "screen out" environmental stimuli:** Students may find it difficult to ignore sounds, smells, or visual distractions in a room, like a loud fan, or constant foot-traffic nearby.

♦ **Inability to concentrate:** Students may be easily distracted and have difficulty focusing on a single task for long periods of time or remembering verbal directions, due to problems with short-term memory.

♦ **Inability to coordinate multiple tasks and deadlines:** Both medication and illness can distort time perception. Prioritizing assignments and meeting deadlines, or adjusting to changes in class schedules or deadlines, can become difficult.

♦ **Problems communicating with others:** Talking with other students, for example, to get notes, form a study group, or even attempt to make a friend can be an enormous challenge.

♦ **Restlessness, dry mouth, and/or nausea:** These are common side effects of psychiatric medications.

Like students who have learning disabilities, students with psychological disabilities can perform academically, in many cases, with some fairly simple accommodations: [55],[56]

♦ To ease distractions, students can be given seats at the front of the class, far from the door, and take exams in separate, quiet rooms.

♦ A tape recorder or note-taker can ease the fatigue of concentrating throughout the class period.

♦ Breaking down papers, assignments, and exams into smaller units can help students concentrate or finish multiple tasks by a deadline.

Federal Law and Student Accommodation

Two federal laws protect teenagers with disabilities and guarantee their right to a "free and appropriate education" at public expense: Section 504 of the Rehabilitation Act of 1973, and the Individuals with Disabilities Education Act.[57]

Section 504

Section 504 protects students who have any physical or mental impairment that "substantially limits one or more major life activities."[58] It is intended to "level the playing field" by removing barriers that prevent students from getting an education.[58] Most students who are covered under Section 504 are taught in a regular classroom, with accommodations. Section 504 reads, in part:

> No otherwise qualified individual with a disability in the United States . . . shall, solely by reason of her or his disability, be excluded from participation in, be denied the benefits of, or be subjected to discrimination under any program or activity receiving Federal financial assistance. (Section 504, 29 U.S.C. §794)

Unlike other programs, "504 status" does not depend on having a particular disability; impairment in **any** major life activity—such as learning or socialization—is grounds for gaining this status.[57,58,59] It is commonly used to help students who do not qualify for special education programs, but still need accommodations to function in regular classrooms.[60]

A "504 plan" is an agreement between the student's family and the school district about what accommodations the student requires to attend school. These plans are a way to tell school staff what to do to help a student from day to day, or how to give emergency assistance.

To set up a 504 plan, ask to speak to your district's 504 plan coordinator. Make sure to put your agreement in writing, as school staff change throughout the year; a written document will ensure that both parents and new school staff understand what the student needs and how it should be provided.

Here are some accommodations that might be included in a 504 plan: [59]

♦ **Physical accommodations,** like providing a quiet area for study, or a standing work station

- ♦ **Instructional accommodations,** like providing written directions on a chalk board or copied in an assignment book by the student and initialed by the teacher

- ♦ **Behavioral accommodations,** such as having a reward system or incentives chart for work and behavior, or making student contracts about behavior

The Individuals with Disabilities Education Act (IDEA)

Created in 1975, Part B of the IDEA includes a set of comprehensive rules and regulations for ensuring that children with disabilities get an adequate education.[57] It requires that all children with disabilities ages 3–21 have access to a free, appropriate public education in the "least restrictive environment" possible.[3,57,63] In other words, students with disabilities should be educated in regular classrooms with supplemental aids and services, such as adaptations to classroom materials, special materials or equipment, including assistive technology, or an individual instructional assistant, if at all possible.[64]

The law requires that IDEA students be educated with their peers, if possible. If these students are removed from their regular classrooms, the school must ensure that they are placed with students from regular classes for non-academic work and extracurricular activities.[64] These students are entitled to accommodation in non-academic classes as well, such as music, art, home economics, or shop.[65] Most children with serious emotional disorders are placed in special education classrooms, and comprise 8.7 percent of all children in special education.[3]

In general, a student who might be covered by IDEA will be evaluated by a school or district eligibility team. If parents are not satisfied with the evaluation, they may either appeal the decision or obtain an independent evaluation and request another meeting, based on the new evaluation.[65]

Once a student is deemed eligible for special education, parents and school representatives meet to create a two-part Individualized Education Plan (IEP). The first part is the "accommodations page," which states what the school district will do to accommodate the student, including what services it will provide, what classroom setting the student will be in, and what other special education resources will be available. Examples of accommodations are as follows:

♦ Providing rooms where students could take a time-out or calm themselves, and procedures for letting students take time out of class

♦ Reducing the number of courses required for graduation

♦ Arranging to let students complete work missed due to symptoms or hospitalization

♦ Providing access to resources like school nurses, social workers, vocational education, or transportation[65,57]

The second part of the document is "goals and objectives," which detail what the student should be able to do by the end of the year and what intermediate steps the student must reach to attain those goals. For students with psychiatric illnesses, these plans often include both behavioral and academic objectives, as these students may need help with both types of skills in order to succeed in school. Learning appropriate social skills through school activities or via social skills groups or peer mentoring can be invaluable to a student who has been hospitalized or homebound.[57]

The goals need to be specific and broken down into achievable steps. For example, an objective like "Joe will comply with the teacher's instructions 9 times out of 10" is useless because there is no mention of why Joe is not paying attention, or how he is supposed to improve his behavior. Appropriate goals state ways that the student and teacher will work to change the student's behavior. If Joe has been ignoring his teacher because he is frustrated with the fast pace of the class, one of Joe's goals might be, "Joe will take a time-out for 5 to 10 minutes when he is overwhelmed."[65]

Students with psychiatric disabilities are generally highly intelligent and can do advanced work, given appropriate accommodations. In fact, many students in gifted and talented programs have IEPs. According to the U.S. Department of Education, "Each child who is evaluated for a suspected learning disability must be measured against his or her own expected performance, and not against some arbitrary general standard."[66] In other words, gifted students with psychiatric disabilities should be expected to excel. To keep a student challenged, despite his or her disability, the IEP may need to include academic options that can be adapted to the student's periods of hospitalization or absence from school, such as distance learning or independent study.[57]

Alternative Programs

Though many students with psychiatric disabilities flourish in traditional classrooms or in special education classes, some students will need extra help—or more flexible arrangements—to succeed. In 1998, 3,380 public alternative schools around the country served about 1 percent of all public school students.[62] Generally, these schools follow the same curriculum as other schools but employ alternate methods of instruction. Other students attend private residential schools that specialize in educating students with mental illnesses. Finally, many students prefer to study at home, with parents or a special tutor, for a General Equivalency Diploma instead of a regular high school diploma.[57]

Re-Entering School After an Absence

Some students with mental illnesses will need to withdraw from school for weeks or months at a time. The transition back to school is a critical time for these teenagers. They may feel embarrassed about or ashamed of being in a psychiatric hospital, and they may feel sleepy, nervous, or nauseated because of their medications. It is very easy for these teens to feel alienated and frightened and to believe that they cannot cope.[57]

For many students, it is easier to restart school gradually, rather than diving headfirst into a full day of classes with their peers. For example, they may begin with home instruction, then start attending a resource room or half-days at school. When the change is gradual, students, parents, and teachers have the opportunity to see how much stress the student can handle, and can give the student a "fallback" position if school becomes too hard to handle.[57]

Discipline

Schools need to tread carefully where students covered by the IDEA are concerned. The IDEA states that students with disabilities are subject to the same rules and discipline as other students—unless the problem is the result of the student's disability. A student who flies into a rage in class would normally be disciplined, but if the rage is a result of that student's bipolar disorder, the school would **not** be able to expel the student.[67] An exception to this policy is students who carry firearms or knowingly bring illegal drugs to school. In these cases, the school may order a temporary change of placement for up to 45 days, while the parents and school staff change the student's IEP plan. Also, as schools need to protect other students and school staff, students can be moved into more restrictive conditions if their behavior threatens themselves or others.[57]

When a student covered by the IDEA is disciplined, schools have 10 days to make a functional behavior assessment (FBA) and develop an intervention plan. The point of the FBA is to look at the root cause of the behavior, not just the act itself; for example students who are frightened, frustrated, bored, or overstimulated may all throw their books on the floor, but for very different reasons.[68] Once the team figures out what function the behavior is fulfilling, the team can find other behaviors that will serve the same function and reduce the student's opportunities to engage in bad behavior. For example, frightened students can learn to raise their hands and can be escorted to a quiet room; bored students can be given more challenging assignments or change tasks more often.[57,63]

Just as the IDEA calls for education in the "least restrictive environment," intervention plans should advocate the most positive, inclusive, and unintrusive ways of changing the student's behavior as possible.[68] In many cases, a student's problem behavior can be stopped by changing the behavior plan or putting that student into a more restrictive setting, without suspending or expelling the student.

The Transition to Adulthood

Eligible students can receive special education services until they obtain a regular high school diploma, or until age 21.[57,64] Eventually, though, students must prepare to leave school. According to the 1997 amendments to the IDEA, a transition plan must be developed by the time a student is 16 years old.[64] This plan can help students move from high school to jobs, college, independent living, or some other role in the community with a minimum of stress or worry.[64] Examples of transition services are classes, job training, instruction in daily living skills, community service, or working with a mentor on a job.[57,64]

Many students with psychiatric disabilities turn 18 while they are still in school and still covered by the IDEA. In some parts of the country, school districts designate 18 year olds as "self-advocates" and make them responsible for their own services. However, students who are considered self-advocates can designate someone to advocate for them, such as a parent or a professional advocate for the disabled.[57,64]

Making the Transition to College

Some colleges have transition programs to help students with disabilities plan for college.

Colorado Mountain College offers a checklist with items like the following:

♦ At the time I apply to college, my psycho-educational assessment will be less than three years old.

♦ I can describe my disability in detail.

♦ I know the kinds of accommodations that will provide me with an equal opportunity to succeed at college.[71]

If a college or university requires standardized tests for admission — such as the Scholastic Aptitude Test (SAT)—students can seek accommodation for their psychiatric disabilities from the Educational Testing Service (ETS). However, ETS requires extensive documentation of the disability (see "Resources," pg. 31 for more information).

Apart from classroom accommodation similar to what 504-plan students receive, the U.S. Department of Education's Office of Civil Rights (OCR) lists several ways that colleges can accommodate students. OCR's recommendations include making "changes in the length of time permitted for the completion of degree requirements, substitution of specific courses required for the completion of degree requirements, and adaptation of the manner in which specific courses are conducted."[70]

Though institutions of higher learning are not allowed to ask applicants about their disabilities, use tests that bar people with disabilities, exclude disabled students from any course of study, or make policies that adversely affect students with disabilities, schools may ask that applicants voluntarily disclose their disabilities during the application process, or before matriculation, and can require documentation of any disability the student discloses.[55,69] Let your college-bound students know that they can voluntarily disclose their disabilities and request accommodation at any time; there is no "cut-off" point for revealing one's disability. As with the 504 plan, there are numerous accommodations that colleges can make (for more information on mental health on campus, see EDC's *Campus Mental Health Issues: Best Practices—A Guide for Colleges* monograph).

Summary

Mental illness is a serious barrier to learning in American secondary schools. Early recognition of symptoms, prompt referrals to care, accessible counseling, and comprehensive prevention programs can help students avoid some of the anguish of mental illness. Institutional support and clear behavioral guidelines can help students with psychiatric disabilities achieve their academic potential and live full lives in their communities.

Resources

Mental Illness

The Bazelon Center for Mental Health Law
Web: http://www.bazelon.org/children.html

This site features information on several aspects of mental health law, including special education, custody issues, and managed health care.

Center for Mental Health Services
Phone: (800) 789-CMHS (2647)
Fax: (301) 984-8796
Web: http://www.mentalhealth.org/

This program of the U.S. Department of Health and Human Services provides information on child and adolescent mental health, treatment, and policy. The site features information on suicide prevention at http://www.mentalhealth.org/suicideprevention/concerned.htm.

Health, Mental Health, and Safety in Schools
Web: http://www.schoolhealth.org/hmhs.htm
Web: http://www.nationalguidelines.org/

The Health, Mental Health, and Safety in Schools newsletter is a collaborative effort and collaboration of organizations and individuals advocating for the physical, mental, and social health of school-age children. The project is supported through a cooperative agreement between the Maternal and Child Health Bureau of the Health Resources and Services Administration, the American Academy of Pediatrics, and the National Association for School Nurses. This initiative is also supporting the development of a compendium of guidelines on a range of issues that impact the overall health, mental health, and safety of students and staff enrolled and working in elementary, middle/junior high, and high schools. The draft guidelines were developed by more than 300 health, education, and safety professionals from more than 30 different national organizations, as well as parents and other supporters.

The Health, Mental Health, and Safety in Schools project is directed by the input of a Central Steering Committee, a governing body comprised of more than 20 leading national health and education organizations. The guidelines are being developed by 14 panels of experts in health, safety, and education, representing varied professions and locations from across the country. The public will be invited to provide input to the final compendium, which will be made available through various publications and the Internet.

The Suicide Prevention Advocacy Network USA (SPAN USA)
Phone: (888) 649-1366
Web: http://www.spanusa.org/

SPAN USA is a not-for-profit 501(c)(3) national organization dedicated to creating an effective national suicide prevention strategy. SPAN USA links the energy of those bereaved by suicide with the expertise of leaders in science, business, government, and public service to achieve the goal of significantly reducing the national rate of suicide by the year 2010.

American Association of Suicidology (AAS)
4201 Connecticut Avenue, NW, Suite 408
Washington, DC 20008
Phone: (202) 237-2280
Fax: (202) 237-2282
Web: http://www.suicidology.org/

The AAS is a not-for-profit organization dedicated to the understanding and prevention of suicide. The organization's Web site is designed as a resource for anyone concerned about suicide, including AAS members, suicide researchers, therapists, prevention specialists, survivors of suicide, and people who are themselves in crisis.

The National Alliance for the Mentally Ill (NAMI)
Phone: (800) 950-NAMI (6264)
Web: http://www.nami.org/

NAMI is a national advocacy and support group and an information clearinghouse for people with mental illnesses and their families and friends.

Educational Issues

Educational Testing Service (ETS)
Web: http://www.ets.org/distest/psyplcy.html#ets

For students with disabilities who are taking the SAT and other standardized ETS tests, ETS provides online "Guidelines for Documentation of Psychiatric Disabilities in Adolescents and Adults."

Learning Disabilities Online
Web: http://www.ldonline.org/index.html

This site offers information on coping with learning disabilities that stem from childhood and adolescent mental illness.

The Sargent Center for Psychiatric Rehabilitation
Boston University
940 Commonwealth Avenue West
Boston, MA 02215
Phone: (617) 353-3549
Fax: (617) 353-7700
TTY: (617) 353-7701
Web: http://www.bu.edu/sarpsych/jobschool/

The Sargent Center provides practical information about psychiatric disabilities, the Americans with Disabilities Act, and other education and employment issues for teaching staff, students, and people with disabilities in the workforce.

Americans With Disabilities Act Home Page
U.S. Department of Justice
Web: http://www.usdoj.gov:80/crt/ada/adahom1.htm

This site contains links to publications on compliance with the Americans with Disabilities Act.

School Violence and Suicide

National Center for Injury Prevention and Control (NCIPC)
Mailstop K65
4770 Buford Highway NE
Atlanta, GA 30341-3724
Phone: (770) 488-1506
Fax: (770) 488-1667
E-mail: OHCINFO@cdc.gov
Web: http://www.cdc.gov/ncipc/

NCIPC provides information on preventing youth violence and suicide. The site contains numerous links to informative publications, such as *Youth Violence: A Report of the Surgeon General* (http://www.surgeongeneral.gov/library/youthviolence) and *Early Warning, Timely Response: A Guide to Safe Schools,* a manual on school violence prevention (http://www.air. org/cecp/guide/ Default.htm).

Related EDC Publications

The following publications are available from:

Health and Human Development Programs
Education Development Center, Inc.
55 Chapel Street, Newton, MA 02458-1060
Phone: (617) 618-2287   **Fax:** (617) 527-4096
E-mail: hhdmail@edc.org

Campus Mental Health Issues: Best Practices—Guide for Colleges
By: Meg Muckenhoupt, Sc.M.
ISBN: 0-89292-256-7

This booklet describes the challenges that student mental health issues pose to colleges and universities, models mental health practices being used at some schools, and offers advice to student affairs and residence life staff, faculty, police, family members, and fellow students on assisting a student who may be suffering from a mental health problem. For a copy of this publication, send $15 plus $3 handling to the address above, marked "Attn: Campus Mental Health Issues."

Health Is Academic: A Guide to Coordinated School Health Programs
Web: http://www2.edc.org/HealthIsAcademic/

This comprehensive guide defines coordinated school health programs and discusses how they contribute to the health and educational achievement of all students, as well as how to implement them. For information on *Health Is Academic,* visit the Web site or contact the address above.

Teenage Health Teaching Modules (THTM)
Web: http://www2.edc.org/thtm/special.htm

THTM is a comprehensive school health education program. Two of the modules address violence prevention: *Aggressors, Victims, and Bystanders: Thinking and Acting to Prevent Violence* for grades 6–8 and *Violence Prevention Curriculum for Adolescents* for grades 9 and 10. Other titles (e.g., *Living with Feelings and Handling Stress* for grades 9 and 10) may be of interest as well. For information on THTM, visit the Web site or contact the address above.

Preventing Injuries and Violence in Schools: New Resources for Public Health Professionals
Web: www.childrenssafetynetwork.org

This four-page information sheet describes the extent of children's injuries at or on the way to and from school, the role of public health professionals, and new resources for prevention activities. Resources include new school health guidelines and initiatives from federal agencies and professional organizations, directories of key federal and national programs, and organizations and research centers that can assist in school injury prevention.

References

[1] Kessler, R.C. et al. (1999). "Social consequences of psychiatric disorders, I: Educational attainment." *American Journal of Psychiatry* 152 (7): 1026–32.

[2] U.S. Surgeon General's Office (2000). *Mental Health: A Report of the Surgeon General, Chapter 3: Children and Mental Health.* Washington, DC: U.S. Department of Health and Human Services. Available online at http://www.surgeongeneral.gov/library/mentalhealth/toc.html#chapter3.

[3] Scallet, L. et al. (2000). *Enhancing Youth Services.* National Association of Psychiatric Health Systems. Available online at http://www.naphs.org/youth_services/lewinpaper.html.

[4] Weissman, M. et al. (1997). Offspring of depressed parents: 10 years later. *Archives of General Psychiatry, 54,* 932–940.

[5] Angold, A., Costello, E., & Erkanli, A. (1999). Comorbidity. *Journal of Child Psychology and Psychiatry and Allied Disciplines, 40*(1), 57–87.

[6] Christie, K. et al. (1988). Epidemiological evidence for early onset of mental disorders and higher risk of drug abuse in young adults. *American Journal of Psychiatry, 145*(8), 971–975.

[7] U.S. Surgeon General's Office (2000). *Mental Health: A Report of the Surgeon General.* Washington, DC: U.S. Department of Health and Human Services. Available online at http://www.surgeongeneral.gov/library/mentalhealth/home.html

[8] Adelman, H. (1998). School counseling, psychological, and social services. In E. Marx & S. Wooley (Eds.), *Health Is Academic: A Guide to Coordinated School Health Programs.* New York: Teachers College Press.

[9] Reschly, D. (2000). The present and future status of school psychology in the United States. *School Psychology Review, 29*(4), 507–522.

[10] Urbaniak, J. (1999). *American Counseling Association Special Message: School counselors' caseloads grow 9.3 percent*. Alexandria, VA: American Counseling Association. Available online at http://www.counseling.org/urgent/special91399.html.

[11] National Alliance for the Mentally Ill (2000). *Facts About Mental Illness*. Washington, DC: National Alliance for the Mentally Ill. Available online at http://www.nami.org/fact.htm.

[12] American Psychiatric Association (1994). *Diagnostic and Statistical Manual of Mental Disorders, Fourth Edition*. Washington, DC: Author.

[13] Kaufmann, C. (1999). An introduction to the mental health consumer movement. In A. Horvitz & T. Scheid (Eds.), *A Handbook for the Study of Mental Health*. Cambridge, UK: Cambridge University Press.

[14] Faraone, S. & Biederman, J. (1998). Depression: A family affair. *The Lancet, 351*(9097), 158.

[15] Geller, B. & Luby, J. (1997). Child and adolescent bipolar disorder: A review of the past 10 years. *Journal of the American Academy of Child and Adolescent Psychiatry, 36*(9), 1168–1176.

[16] Newman, D. et al. (1996). Psychiatric disorders in a birth cohort of young adults: Prevalence, comorbidity, clinical significance, and new case incidence from ages 11 to 21. *Journal of Consulting and Clinical Psychology, 64*(3), 552–562.

[17] National Clearinghouse on Families & Youth (1996). *Supporting Your Adolescent: Tips for Parents*. Washington, DC: U.S. Department of Health and Human Services; Administration for Children and Families; Administration on Children, Youth, and Families; Family and Youth Services Bureau. Available online at http://www.ncfy.com/supporti.htm.

[18] Blau, G. M. (1996). Adolescent suicide and depression. In G.M. Blau & T. P. Gullotta (Eds.), *Adolescent Dysfunctional Behavior: Causes, Interventions, and Prevention*. Thousand Oaks, CA: Sage Publications.

[19] Freydenberg, E. (1997). *Adolescent Coping: Theoretical and Research Perspectives.* New York: Routledge.

[20] Group for the Advancement of Psychiatry Committee on Adolescence (1996). *Adolescent Suicide.* Washington, DC: American Psychiatric Press.

[21] McIntosh, J. (1999). *1998 Official Final Statistics U.S.A. SUICIDE.* Washington, DC: The American Association of Suicidology. Available online at http://www.suicidology.org/index.html.

[22] Andrews, J. & Lewingson, P. (1992). Suicidal attempts among older adolescents: Prevalence and co-occurrence with psychiatric disorders. *Journal of the American Academy of Child and Adolescent Psychiatry, 31*(4), 655–662.

[23] Capuzzi, D. & Gross, D. (1989). "I don't want to live": suicidal behavior. In D. Capuzzi & D. Gross (Eds.), *Youth at Risk: A Resource for Counselors, Teachers, and Parents.* Alexandria, VA: American Association for Counseling and Development.

[24] National Alliance for the Mentally Ill (2001). *Teenage Suicide.* Available online at http://www.nami.org/helpline/teensuicide.html.

[25] National Center for Injury Prevention & Control (2000). *Best Practices of Youth Violence Prevention: A Sourcebook for Community Action.* Atlanta, GA: Center for Disease Control and Prevention, National Center for Injury Prevention and Control. Available online at http://www.cdc.gov/ncipc/dvp/bestpractices.htm#Download.

[26] American Academy of Child and Adolescent Psychiatry (1999). *1999 Violence Fact Sheet.* Washington, DC: American Academy of Child and Adolescent Psychiatry. Available online at http://www.aacap.org/web/ aacap/info_families/NationalFacts/99ViolFctSh.htm.

[27] Lumsden, L. (2001). Trends and issues: School safety and violence prevention. *ERIC Clearinghouse on Educational Management.* Eugene, OR: College of Education, University of Oregon.

[28] Mazza, J. & Overstreet, S. (2000). Children and adolescents exposed to community violence: A mental health perspective for school psychologists. *School Psychology Review, 29*(1), 86–101.

[29] Center for Effective Collaboration and Practice (2000). *Early Warning, Timely Response: A Guide to Safe Schools.* Washington, DC: CECP. Available online at http://www.air.org/cecp/ guide/ Default.htm.

[30] Surgeon General (2000). *Youth Violence: A Report of the Surgeon General.* Washington, DC: U.S. Department of Health and Human Services.

[31] New Mexico State University Counseling Center (2000). *Crisis and Referrals.* Las Cruces, NM: New Mexico State University. Available online at http://www.nmsu.edu/~counsel/ homepage.html#REFERRAL.

[32] Washington State University Counseling Services (2000). *Information for WSU Faculty Responding to Students in Distress.* Pullman, WA: Washington State University. Available online at http://www.counsel.wsu.edu/csweb/Counseling_Faculty.htm.

[33] University of British Columbia Counseling Services (2000). *Identifying and Referring "At-Risk" Students: A Guide for Faculty and Staff.* Vancouver, BC, Canada: University of British Columbia. Available online at http://www.student-services.ubc.ca/ counselling/consult/atrisk.htm.

[34] Personal Counseling and Career Service Center, Brooklyn College (2000). *How to Identify, Assist and Refer Students with Personal Problems and/or Disruptive Behavior: Guide for Brooklyn College Faculty and Staff.* Brooklyn, NY: Brooklyn College. Available online at http://depthome.brooklyn.cuny.edu/ career/FACRFRL.HTM.

[35] Counseling Center, George Mason University (2000). *Recognizing and Responding to Students in Emotional Distress.* Fairfax, VA: George Mason University. Available online at http://www.gmu.edu/departments/csdc/dist.html.

[36] Student Counseling Services, Illinois State University (2000). *A Guide for Faculty.* Normal, IL: Illinois State University. Available online at http://www.ilstu.edu/depts/CCS/scs99_cs/ f_guide.htm.

[37] Hoover, A. et al. (1999). Prevention and intervention strategies with children of alcoholics. *Pediatrics, 103* [suppl], 1112–1121.

[38] Hellerstedt, W., Fee, R., & Stevens, A. (2001): *Minor Consent and Confidentiality and Adolescent Health in Minnesota.* University of Minnesota Extension. Available online at http://www.extension.umn. edu/distribution/ familydevelopment/components/7286-11.html.

[39] Evans, S. (1999). Mental health services in schools: Utilization, effectiveness, and consent. *Clinical Psychology Review, 19*(2), 165–178.

[40] Gullat, D. & Stockton, C. (2000). Recognizing and reporting suspected child abuse. *American Secondary Education, 29*(1), 19–26.

[41] Kendell, Nicole (2000). *Issue Brief: School-Based Mental Health.* Health Policy Tracking Service, National Conference of State Legislatures. Available online at http://www.stateserv.hpts.org/ HPTS2001/issueb2001.nsf/cd5fe07d402115ac852564f0007cb093/ 0cbf250cc509837a85256784004e1328?OpenDocument.

[42] Brant, R. and Brant, J. (1998). Child and adolescent therapy. In L. Lifson & R. Simon (Eds.), *The Mental Health Practitioner and the Law.* Cambridge, MA: Harvard University Press.

[43] Kubiszyn, T. (1999). Integrating health and mental health services in schools: Psychologists collaborating with primary care providers. *Clinical Psychology Review, 19*(2), 177–198.

[44] Quinn, K. & McDougal, J. (1998). A mile wide and a mile deep: Comprehensive interventions for children and youth with emotional and behavioral disorders and their families. *School Psychology Review, 27*(2), 191–203.

[45] Morone, J., Kilbreth, E., & Langwell, K. (January/February, 2001). Back to school: A health care strategy for youth: The school-based health centers are controversial—but they might just fit in the political temper of our times. *Health Affairs.*

[46] English, A. (1999). Health care for the adolescent alone: A legal landscape. In J. Blustein, C. Levine, & N. Dubler (Eds.), *The Adolescent Alone: Decision Making in Health Care in the United States.* New York: Cambridge University Press.

[47] Adelman, H. & Taylor, Linda (1999). Mental health in schools and system restructuring. *Clinical Psychology Review, 19*(2), 136–163.

[48] Pfeiffer, S. & Reddy, L. (1998). School-based mental health programs in the United States: Present status and a blueprint for the future. *School Psychology Review, 27*(1), 84–96.

[49] Durlak, J. (1998). Common risk and protective factors in successful prevention programs. *American Journal of Orthopsychiatry, 68*(4), 512–520.

[50] Durlak, J. & Wells, A. (1997). Primary prevention mental health programs for children and adolescents: A meta-analytic review. *American Journal of Community Psychology, 25*(2), 115–152.

[51] Greenberg, M. T., Domitrovich, C., and Bumbarger, B. (2001). The prevention of mental disorders in school-aged children: current state of the field. *Prevention & Treatment, 4*(1).

[52] National Institute of Mental Health (1998). *Priorities for Prevention Research.* NIH Publication No. 98-4321. Washington, DC: U.S. Department of Health and Human Services.

[53] Promotion and Prevention, Mental Health Branch, Department of Aged and Health Care (2001). *Mind Matters: Understanding Mental Illness.* Carlton, South Victoria, Australia: Curriculum Corporation. Available online at http://online.curriculum.edu.au/mindmatters/new/display.asp?pg=/resources/understdg.htm.

[54] Burns, B. et al. (Fall, 1995). DataWatch: Children's mental health service use across service sectors. *Health Affairs.*

[55] Dean of Students (2000). *College Students with Disabilities Desk Reference for Faculty & Staff.* Lubbock, TX: Texas Tech University.

[56] Web Site Advisory Board and Staff (1999). *Handling Your Psychiatric Disability at Work and School.* Boston, MA: Center for Psychiatric Rehabilitation, Sargent Center for Psychiatric Rehabilitation, Boston University. Available online at http://www.bu.edu/ sarpsych/jobschool/.

[57] Waltz, M. (2000). *Bipolar Disorders: A Guide to Helping Children and Adolescents.* Cambridge, MA: O'Reilly.

[58] Rosenfeld, S. (2001). Section 504 and IDEA: Basic similarities and differences. *LD Online Newsletter.* Available online at http://www.ldonline.org/ld_indepth/legal_legislative/edlaw504.html.

[59] Blazer, B. (1999). Developing 504 classroom accommodation plans: A collaborative systematic parent-student-teacher approach. *Teaching Exceptional Children, 32*(2).

[60] Alaska Transition Initiative (2001). *What Is a 504 Plan? Typically Asked Questions.* Available online at http://www.sesa.org/ati/504.html

[61] Dwyer, K. & Bernstein, R. (1998). Mental health in the schools: Linking islands of hope in a sea of despair. *School Psychology Review, 27*(2) 277–286.

[62] The Center for Health and Health Care in Schools (Summer, 2000). SBHCs and alternative schools: A good match. *Access.* Available online at http://www.healthinschools.org/pubs/access/Summer 2000.asp.

[63] Gable, R. et al. (2000). *Addressing Student Problem Behavior.* Washington, DC: Center for Effective Collaboration and Practice, American Institutes for Research. Available online at http://www.air.org/cecp/fba/problembehavior3/main3.htm.

[64] Levin, C., Villegas, A., & Wrigley, J. (1999). *Special Education: A Guide for Parents and Advocates. Step 4: Placement in the Least Restrictive Environment (LRE).* Portland, OR: Oregon Advocacy Center. Available online at http://www.oradvocacy.org/step4.htm.

[65] Learning Disabilities Association (2001). *How to Participate Effectively in the IEP Process.* Pittsburgh, PA: Author. Available online at http://www.ldanatl.org/pamphlets/iep.shtml.

[66] Letter of Clarification from Thomas Hehir, Director, Office of Special Education Programs, to Ms. Patricia M. Lillie, and Rebecca Felton, Ph.D., Learning Disabilities Association of North Carolina, Inc., dated April 5, 1995.

[67] NASW School Social Workers (1999). *Student Discipline and IDEA*. Washington, DC: The National Association of Social Workers, School Social Work Section. Available online at http://www.naswdc.org/ sections/SSW/hottopics/ sdiscipline.htm.

[68] Clark, J. (1998). *Functional Behavioral Assessment and Behavioral Intervention Plans: Implementing the Student Discipline Provisions of IDEA '97*. Washington, DC: The National Association of Social Workers, School Social Work Section. Available online at http://www.naswdc.org/sections/ SSW/schclark.htm.

[69] Evans, M. (2000). *Counseling Center Referral Guide*. Eugene, OR: University of Oregon Counseling and Testing Center. Available online at http://darkwing.uoregon.edu/~counsel/ consult.htm.

[70] Flygare, Thomas (2000). *Students with Learning and Psychiatric Disabilities: New Challenges for Colleges and Universities*. Washington, DC: National Association of College and University Attorneys.

[71] Colorado Mountain College Disability Services (2001). *Checklist: Before Transitioning to College*. Glenwood Springs, CO: Author. Available online at http://www.coloradomtn.edu/studentsvcs/ disabilitysvcs/transition.html.

[72] National Center for Injury Prevention and Control (2001). *Youth Violence in the United States*. Atlanta, GA: Centers for Disease Control and Prevention. Available online at http://www.cdc.gov/ncipc/ dvp/yvpt/newfacts.htm.

[73] National Center for Injury Prevention and Control (2001). *Leading Causes of Death Reports*. Atlanta, GA: Centers for Disease Control and Prevention. Available online at http://webapp.cdc.gov/ sasweb/ncipc/leadcaus.html.

[74] Silverman, J. et al. (2001). Dating violence against adolescent girls and associated substance use, unhealthy weight control, sexual risk behavior, pregnancy, and suicidality. *Journal of the American Medical Association, 286*(5), 572–579.

[75] O'Carroll, P. et al. (1994). *Suicide Contagion and the Reporting of Suicide: Recommendations from a National Workshop.* Atlanta, GA: Centers for Disease Control and Prevention. *MMWR* 43(RR-6), 9–18. Available online at http://wonder.cdc.gov/wonder/prevguid/m0031539/m0031539.asp

[76] National Education Association (2001). *NEA Crisis Communication Guide and Toolkit.* Washington, DC: National Education Association. Available online at http://www.nea.org/crisis/b1home.html.